The Salad

Cookbook

50 Easy & Satisfying Recipes That

Make a Healthy and Delicious Meal

ALFREDO TOSCANA

The information in following pages is broadly considered a truthful and accurate account of facts and as such, any inattention, use, or misuse of the information in question by the reader will render any resulting actions solely under their purview. There are no scenarios in which the publisher or the original author of this work can be in any fashion deemed liable for any hardship or damages that may befall them after undertaking information described herein.

Additionally, the information in the following pages is intended only for informational purposes, should thus be thought of as universal. As befitting its nature, it is presented without assurance regarding its prolonged validity or interim quality. Trademarks that are mentioned are done without written consent and can in no way be considered an endorsement from the trademark holder.

Additionally, the information in the following pages is intended only for informational purposes and should thus be thought of as universal. As befitting its nature, it is presented without assurance regarding its prolonged validity or interim quality. Trademarks that are mentioned are done without written consent and can in no way be considered an endorsement from the trademark holder.

Table of contents

VEGETABLE SALADS

With the knowledge already obtained of the food value of the vegetables that are generally used as ingredients in the vegetable salads, the housewife ought to have no difficulty in determining whether she is giving her family a salad that is high or low in food value.

For instance, she should know that the food value of a plain lettuce or cucumber salad is lower than that of one made from potatoes because of the different values in the vegetables used.

Green Vegetable Salad

There are several green vegetables that are much used for salad either alone or with other vegetables. All of them are used in practically the same way, but a point that should not be overlooked if an appetizing salad is desired is that they should always be fresh and crisp when served. Any salad dressing that is preferred may be served with them.

Chief among these green vegetables is lettuce, including the ordinary leaf lettuce, head lettuce, and romaine lettuce, which is not so common as other varieties. Several kinds of endive as well as watercress may also be used for salad.

Mixed Vegetable Salad #1

Ingredients:

- ✓ One pint of cold boiled potatoes cut in slices.
- ✓ 1/3 of the quantity of cold boiled beets cut fine.
- ✓ 1/3 of the quantity of green peas.

Preparation:

- ✓ Sprinkle with the salt and pepper, then pour over it a French dressing made of a saltspoonful of salt, 1 of black pepper, a teaspoonful of onion juice, or grated onion, 3 tablespoonfuls of olive oil and 1 of vinegar.
- ✓ Mix thoroughly and set aside.
- ✓ When is ready to serve spread over it mayonnaise dressing and garnish with slices of beet, cut in shapes, hardboiled egg, and parsley.
- ✓ If made in summer a border of crisp lettuce leaves is an additional garnish.
- ✓ If the quantity of vegetable is increased the amount of dressing must also be doubled or the salad will be dry.

Mix vegetable salad #2

Ingredients:

- ✓ 1 cup finely cut red cabbage
- ✓ 1 cup cold boiled beets
- ✓ 1 cup cold boiled carrots
- ✓ 1 cup cold boiled potatoes
- ✓ 1 cup chopped celery
- ✓ 1/2 cup pimentos
- ✓ 1 head lettuce
- ✓ 1 cup French dressing

Preparation:

- ✓ Soak cabbage in cold water one hour; drain and add beets, carrots and potatoes cut into small pieces, add celery. Mix well, season with the salt and pepper and serve on lettuce leaves.
- ✓ On top put strips of pimento and serve with French dressing, to which may be added one teaspoon onion juice.

Cucumber Salad #1

Besides serving plain slices of cucumber on a lettuce leaf, as may be done at any time, cucumbers may be used as an ingredient in the making of many salads.

Ingredients:

- ✓ 3 medium-sized cucumbers
- ✓ 1 c. diced tomato
- ✓ 1/2 c. diced celery
- ✓ Salad dressing
- ✓ Lettuce
- ✓ 1 pimiento

Preparation:

- ✓ Peel cucumbers cut them into halves, and using a small spoon scoop out cucumbers in chunks, so that a boat-shaped piece of it that is about 1/4 inch thick remains.
- ✓ Dice pieces of cucumber which have been scooped from the center, and place cucumber shells in ice water to make them crisp.

- ✓ Mix diced tomato, celery, cucumber and just before serving drain them carefully so that no liquid remains.

- ✓ Mix with salad dressing, wipe cucumber shells dry, fill them with the salad mixture, and place on salad plates garnished with lettuce leaves.

- ✓ Cut the pimiento into thin strips, and place three or four strips diagonally across the cucumber.
  Sufficient to Serve Six

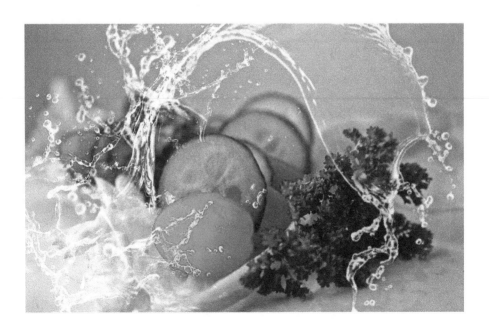

Cucumber Salad #2

Preparation:

- ✓ Pare thickly, from end to end, and lay in ice and water one hour.
- ✓ Wipe them, slice thin, and slice an onion equally thin. Strew salt over them, shake up a few times, cover and let remain in this brine for one hour.
- ✓ Then squeeze or press out every drop of water which has been extracted from the cucumbers.
- ✓ Put into a salad bowl, sprinkle with white pepper and scatter bits of parsley over them. Add enough vinegar to cover.
- ✓ You may slice up an equal quantity of white or red radishes and mix with this salad.

Cucumber Salad #3

Preparation:

- ✓ Peel and slice a cucumber, mix 1/2 a teaspoonful of salt, 1/4 of a teaspoonful of white pepper, and 2 tablespoonfuls of olive oil, stir it well together.
- ✓ Add very gradually 1 tablespoonful of vinegar, stirring it all the time.
- ✓ Put the sliced cucumber into a salad dish and garnish it with nasturtium leaves and flowers.

Cucumber & Tomato Salad

A fresh salad made of cucumbers and tomatoes is always attractive because of contrasting colors of vegetables, and it is at the same time extremely palatable.

When such a salad is to be made, small, firm tomatoes and rather large cucumbers that do not contain very large seeds should be selected.

Preparation:

- ✓ Peel the cucumbers and tomatoes and cut them into slices of any desired thickness.
- ✓ Garnish salad plates with lettuce, and on this place a ring of slices, alternating tomatoes with cucumbers.
- ✓ In the center, put a slice of cucumber or tomato and serve with any desired salad dressing.

Sliced Cucumber & Onion Salad

An attractive way in which to serve sliced cucumbers, and onions. You have to select a single large cucumber for this salad.

Preparation:

- ✓ With a sharp knife, peel skin from the cucumber in narrow strips back to the stem end, but do not cut the strips loose from the end.
- ✓ After the peeling has all been removed, place the cucumber on a board and cut it into thin slices.
- ✓ Place on a small platter, as shown, arrange slices of onion around edge, and pour French dressing over the whole.
- ✓ Dust with paprika and serve.
- ✓ A few slices of cucumber and 1 or 2 slices of onion should be served to each person.

Onion Salad

To persons who are fond of flavor of onions, salad given in accompanying recipe is very agreeable, but it is a wise plan not to serve onions unless everyone who is served is certain to enjoy them... When a salad is made from onions, a mild onion should be selected.

Ingredients:

- ✓ 3 onions
- ✓ French dressing
- ✓ Parsley
- ✓ Lettuce

Preparation:

- ✓ Peel onions and slice them into thin slices.
- ✓ Chop parsley and add it to 1 or 2 tablespoonfuls of French dressing. Use comparatively coarse leaves of lettuce and shred them.
- ✓ Arrange slices of onion on a bed of lettuce, pour French dressing with parsley overall, and serve.

Onion Salad #2

Ingredients:

- ✓ 1 large, boiled onion (Spanish)
- ✓ 3 large, boiled potatoes
- ✓ 1 teaspoonful of parsley
- ✓ Pepper and salt, juice of 1 lemon
- ✓ 2 or 3 tablespoonfuls of olive oil

Preparation:

- ✓ Slice onion and potatoes when quite cold, mix well together with parsley and pepper and salt.
- ✓ Add the lemon juice and oil and mix well.

Tomato Salad #1

Fresh tomatoes make a delightful salad thanks to their appetizing appearance and color. In fact, when tomatoes are placed on a bed of green garnish, nothing can be more delightful. Tomatoes may be served whole on a lettuce leaf or they may be sliced. Then, again, they may be cut from center into sections that can fall part way open. In any of these forms, they may be served with French dressing, mayonnaise, or any cooked salad dressing.

Tomato Salad #2

Ingredients:

- ✓ Six tomatoes
- ✓ One-half cup of mayonnaise dressing
- ✓ The crisp part of one head of lettuce

Preparation:

- ✓ Peel tomatoes and put them on the ice until they are very cold. Make the mayonnaise and stand it on ice until wanted; wash and dry the lettuce.

✓ When ready to serve, cut tomatoes in halves, make twelve little nests with 2 or 3 salad leaves each, arrange on dish, place half a tomato in each nest, put a tablespoonful of mayonnaise on each tomato and serve immediately.

Tomato Salad #3

(With Canned Tomatoes)

Preparation:

✓ Rub through a coarse sieve one can of tomatoes.
✓ Cover with cold water a half box of Cox gelatin and let it stand a half hour or more. Then pour in enough hot water to thoroughly dissolve it.
✓ Then mix with one full pint of strained tomatoes.
✓ Add a little salt. Pour into small round moulds and put in a cool place to harden. Serve on lettuce leaves with mayonnaise dressing.

Tomato Salad #4

Preparation:

- ✓ Select perfectly ripe tomatoes, and peel at least an hour before using.
- ✓ Slice, and place on ice or in a cool place.
- ✓ Serve plain or with lemon juice or sugar as preferred.

Tomato Salad #5

Ingredients:

- ✓ One half small yellow tomato
- ✓ One half red

Preparation:

- ✓ Slice evenly and lay in dish in alternate layers.
- ✓ Powder lightly with sugar and turn over them a cupful of orange juice to a pint of tomato, or if preferred, the juice of lemons may be used instead.
- ✓ Set on ice and cool before serving.

Stuffed Tomato Salad

An attractive salad in which vegetables of almost any kind, fresh or canned, is a stuffed tomato salad. Medium-sized, well-ripened tomatoes are best to select for it. You can use for stuffing celery, radishes, onion, cucumbers, green peas, cooked asparagus, string beans. Any combination of these vegetables will make a satisfactory filling.

Ingredients:

- ✓ 6 medium-sized tomatoes
- ✓ French dressing
- ✓ 1 1/2 c. diced vegetables
- ✓ Mayonnaise dressing

Preparation:

- ✓ Cut out stem and blossom end of tomatoes, hollow out the center to leave a shell. Dice the tomatoes' contents and mix with the other diced vegetables.
- ✓ Marinate diced vegetables with French dressing and put into tomato shells, heaping each one.
- ✓ Place on lettuce leaves and serve with mayonnaise.

FRUIT SALADS

Salads made of fruit are undoubtedly the most delicious to prepare. In addition to being delightful in both appearance and flavor, they afford another means of introducing fruit into the diet. As fruit is decidedly beneficial for all persons with a normal digestion, every opportunity to include it in the diet should be grasped.

Some fruit salads are comparatively bland in flavor while others are much more acid. The mild ones are neither so appetizing nor so beneficial as those which are somewhat tart. Advantage should be taken of the various kinds of fresh fruits during the seasons when they can be obtained, for usually very appetizing salads can be made of them.

However, the family need not be deprived of fruit salads during the winter when fresh fruits cannot be secured, for delicious salads can be made from canned and dried fruits, as well as from bananas and citrus fruits, which are usually found in all markets.

Fruit Salad Dressing

Various dressings may be served with a fruit salad. Usually, the one selected depends on preference of those to whom it is served. However, an excellent dressing for salad of this kind and one that most persons find delicious is made from fruit juices thickened by means of eggs. Whenever a recipe in this Section calls for a fruit salad dressing, this is the one that is intended.

Ingredients:

- ✓ 1/2 c. pineapple, peach, or pear juice
- ✓ 1/2 c. orange juice
- ✓ 1/4 c. lemon juice
- ✓ 1/4 c. sugar
- ✓ 2 eggs

Preparation:

- ✓ Mix fruit juices, add the sugar, beat the eggs slightly, and add them. Put the whole into a double boiler and cook until mixture begins to thicken.
- ✓ Remove from fire and beat for a few seconds with a rotary eggbeater. Cool and serve.

Mixed Fruit Salad #1

Mix of fruits given in the accompanying recipe, makes for sure a good salad, but it need not be adhered to strictly. If one or more of the fruits is not in supply, it may be omitted and some other used. In case canned pineapple is used for the salad, the juice from the fruit may be utilized in making a fruit salad dressing.

Ingredients:

- ✓ 1 grapefruit
- ✓ 2 oranges
- ✓ 1 banana
- ✓ 2 apples
- ✓ 2 slices pineapple
- ✓ Salad dressing
- ✓ Lettuce

Preparation:
- ✓ Prepare the grapefruit and oranges according to the directions previously given.
- ✓ Slice banana crosswise into 1/4-inch slices and cut each slice into four sections.

- ✓ Dice apples and cut the pineapple in narrow wedge-shaped pieces. Mix the fruit just before serving.
- ✓ Add the salad dressing, which may be fruit-salad dressing, French dressing, or some other desirable salad dressing, by mixing it with the fruit or merely pouring it over the top.
- ✓ Serve on salad plates garnished with lettuce leaves.
- ✓ Place a maraschino cherry on top.
- ✓ Sufficient to Serve Six.

Mixed Fruit Salad #2

Preparation:

- ✓ Take sweet, ripe oranges, apples, bananas, grapes.
- ✓ Peel the oranges, quarter them, and remove skin and pips. Peel and core apples and cut into thin slices.
- ✓ Wash and dry the grapes and remove from stalks.
- ✓ Skin and slice the bananas. Put prepared fruit into a glass dish in alternate layers. Squeeze the juice from two sweet oranges and pour over the salad.
- ✓ Any other fresh fruit in season may be used for this salad. Castor sugar may be sprinkled over if desired, and cream used in place of the juice.
- ✓ Grated nuts are also a welcome addition.

Mixed Fruit Salad #3

Preparation:

- ✓ Slice one pineapple, 3 oranges, and 3 bananas.
- ✓ Pour over it a French mayonnaise, put on the lettuce leaves and serve at once.
- ✓ For those who do not care for the mayonnaise, make a syrup of one cup of sugar and ½ cup of water, boil until thick, add juice of lemon, let slightly cool, then pour over fruit. Let stand on ice for one hour.
- ✓ Another nice dressing is one cup of claret, one-half cup of sugar, and piece of lemon.
- ✓ Always use lemon juice in preference to vinegar in fruit salads. All fruits that go well together may be mixed. This is served just before desert.

Fruit Salad (Iced)

Preparation:

- ✓ Make 1/4 of lemon or orange water ice and stand it aside for at least one or two hours to ripen.
- ✓ Make a fruit salad from stemmed strawberries, sliced bananas cut into tiny bits, a few very ripe cherries, a grated pineapple if you have it, and pulp of four or five oranges.
- ✓ After the water ice is frozen rather hard, pack it in a border mold, put on the lid or cover and bind seam with a strip of muslin dipped in paraffin or suet, and repack to freeze for three or four hours.
- ✓ Sweeten the fruit combination, if you like, add a tablespoonful or two of brandy and sherry, and stand this on the ice until very cold.
- ✓ At serving time, turn the mold of water ice on to a round compote dish, quickly fill the center with fruit salad, garnish the outside with fresh roses or violets, and send at once to the table.

Fruit and Nut Salad

Preparation:

- ✓ Slice 2 bananas, 2 oranges and mix them with ½ cup of English walnuts and the juice of ½ lemon with French dressing.
- ✓ Serve on lettuce leaves.

Hungarian Fruit Salad

Preparation:

- ✓ Mix equal parts of banana, orange, pineapple, grapefruit and one-half cup of chopped nuts.
- ✓ Marinate with French dressing.
- ✓ Fill apple or orange skins with mixture.
- ✓ Arrange on a bed of watercress or lettuce leaves.
- ✓ Sprinkle with paprika.

Russian Fruit Salad

Preparation:

- ✓ Peel and pit some peaches, cut in slices, and add as much sliced pineapple, some apricots, strawberries, and raspberries, put these in a dish.
- ✓ Prepare a syrup of juice of two lemons, two oranges, one cup of water and 1 pound sugar, a half teaspoon of powdered cinnamon, grated rind of lemon, add one cup red wine and a ½ glass of rum.
- ✓ Boil this syrup for five minutes, then pour over the fruit, tossing the fruit from time to time until cool.
- ✓ Place on ice and serve cold.

Summer Mix Fruit Salad

Any agreeable combination of fruits that you can obtained during same season will be suitable for summer mix salad. A combination given in the accompanying recipe includes strawberries, pineapple, and cherries. However, pineapple and cherries may be used alone, or strawberries, pineapple may be used without cherries. Red raspberries may be used to garnish such a salad.

Ingredients:

- ✓ 3/4 c. strawberries, cut into halves
- ✓ 3/4 c. pineapple, cut into dice
- ✓ 3/4 c. sweet cherries, seeded
- ✓ Lettuce
- ✓ Fruit-salad dressing

Preparation:

- ✓ Prepare the fruits just before serving.
- ✓ Put them together, place on salad plates garnished with lettuce, and serve with the fruit-salad dressing.

Filbert & Cherry Salad

If you would like a different way to prepare salad, cherries that have been seeded and then filled with filberts to prove a delightful change. You can serve this salad with dressing at your choice, but fruit-salad dressing makes it especially delicious.

HIGH PROTEIN SALADS

Salads that are made with cheese, eggs, fish, or meat, may be classed as High Protein Salads, for, as has already been learned, these foods are characterized by the protein they contain. Of course, those made almost entirely of meat or fish are higher in this food substance than the others.

However, the salads that contain a combination of cheese and fruit are comparatively high in protein, and supply to the diet what is desirable in the way of a fruit salad.

Egg salad

Ingredients:

- ✓ 6 Eggs
- ✓ 1 Lettuce
- ✓ 1 bunch Watercress
- ✓ Mayonnaise or Salad Dressing
- ✓ 1 Beetroot

Preparation:

- ✓ Put eggs into boiling water and boil fifteen minutes.
- ✓ Plunge into cold water till quite cold, peel, and cut into quarters.
- ✓ Wash and cleanse the watercress and lettuce and cut into pieces.
- ✓ Put a layer of this at the bottom of the bowl, then one of eggs dipped in dressing, then another of lettuce and egg until all are used up, leaving plenty of lettuce for the top.
- ✓ Garnish with sprigs of watercress and slices of beetroot alternately.

Eggplant Salad (Turkish Style)

Preparation:

- ✓ Use small eggplants. Place on end of toasting fork under broiler gas flame until the peel is black. Remove the skin.
- ✓ Eggplant will then be tender; chop with wooden spoon, add lemon juice, parsley chopped fine, olive oil.

Egg Salad with Mayonnaise

Ingredients:

- ✓ 1 lb. of cold boiled potatoes
- ✓ 6 hard-boiled eggs
- ✓ the juice of ½ a lemon, pepper, and salt

Preparation:

- ✓ Cut the potatoes and eggs into slices, dust them with pepper and salt, add the lemon juice, and mix all well together. Cover with mayonnaise, garnish with watercress.

Cheese Salad

Preparation:

- ✓ Put some finely shredded lettuce in a glass dish, and over this put some young sliced onions, mustard and cress, a layer of sliced tomatoes, and two hard-boiled eggs, also sliced.
- ✓ Add salt, pepper, and then over all put a nice layer of grated cheese.
- ✓ Serve with a dressing composed of equal parts of cream, salad oil, and vinegar, into which had been smoothly mixed a little mustard.

Peach & Cream Cheese Salad

A good way of using canned peaches is to combine it with cream cheese for a salad. If a smaller salad is desired, half a peach may be used, and cheese placed on the top of it. Firm yellow peaches are the best ones to use for this dish.

- ✓ Lettuce
- ✓ Salad dressing
- ✓ 8 halves of pecans or walnuts
- ✓ 2 Tb. cream
- ✓ 1/4 tsp. salt
- ✓ 1 pkg. Cream cheese
- ✓ 8 halves canned peaches

Preparation:

- ✓ Mix cream and salt with cheese and shape into balls.
- ✓ Place a ball between 2 peach halves and press them together tightly.
- ✓ Place on garnished salad plates, pour salad dressing over the top, and garnish with two halves of the nuts.
- ✓ If desired, nuts may be chopped and sprinkled over the top. Sufficient to Serve Four.

Pear & Cheese Salad

Ingredients:

- ✓ 2 Tb. cream
- ✓ Lettuce
- ✓ 1/4 tsp. salt
- ✓ 4 halves English walnuts
- ✓ 1 pkg. cream cheese
- ✓ Salad dressing
- ✓ 8 halves canned pears

Preparation:

- ✓ Mix cream and salt with cheese and shape into balls. Place one-half of a pear with the hollow side up on a salad plate garnished with a lettuce leaf and other half with the hollow side down beside it.
- ✓ Put a ball of the cheese in the hollow of the upturned half and press half an English walnut on top of that.
- ✓ Add dressing and serve. French dressing is recommended for this salad.

Macaroni & Cheese Salad

Ingredients:

- ✓ 1/4 lb. Macaroni
- ✓ 1/4 lb. Cheese
- ✓ 1 teaspoonful French Mustard
- ✓ 3 tablespoonsful Oil
- ✓ 3 tablespoonsful Vinegar
- ✓ 1/2 Head of Celery
- ✓ 1/2 Lettuce

Preparation:

- ✓ Boil macaroni or use any cold that may be in larder.
- ✓ Cut it into pieces about three inches long, cut cheese into very thin slices, and cut the celery into very small pieces.
- ✓ Lay these alternately in a bowl with some shredded lettuce. Make a dressing of mustard, oil, vinegar, and pour it over.
- ✓ Garnish with a little beetroot and serve.

Green Pepper & Cheese Salad

Vegetable and cheese mix in form of salad can be made of green pepper and cheese. To make this kind of salad, select firm green peppers, one being sufficient if a large one, can be obtained. Season cream cheese well with paprika and a little additional salt if necessary.

Preparation:

- ✓ Cut the top from pepper, clean out the inside, and pack tight with the cheese.
- ✓ Cut the filled pepper into thin slices, place two or three of these slices on a salad plate garnished with lettuce leaves and serve with French dressing.

FISH SALADS

Fish salad #1

Ingredients:

- ✓ Cold Boiled Fish
- ✓ 1 Lettuce, salad Dressing
- ✓ 1 Egg

Preparation:

- ✓ Flake up the fish free from skin and bone.
- ✓ Wash and dry lettuce and shred it up, mix fish with salad dressing. Put a layer of lettuce at the bottom of the bowl, then one of fish and dressing.
- ✓ Garnish with hard boiled eggs cut into slices.

Fish Salad #2

Ingredients:

- ✓ Salmon or Tuna fish
- ✓ 1 can salmon or tuna fish
- ✓ 1 cupful shredded cabbage or sliced celery

Preparation:

- ✓ Drain the oil from fish. Remove the bone and bits of skin.
- ✓ Add cabbage or celery, and Mayonnaise or Cream Salad Dressing.
- ✓ Arrange on lettuce and garnish as desired.

- ✓ If cream Dressing is used with salmon, oil drained from salmon may be used for fat of Cream Dressing.
- ✓ The salmon may be marinated before adding the other ingredients. When this is done, salad dressing may be omitted. Salmon contains so much fat that it is not well to add more oil after marinating.

Fish Salad #3

Preparation:

- ✓ Cut in small pieces any cold dressed fish, turbot or salmon are the best suited.
- ✓ Mix it with half a pint of small salad, and a lettuce cut small, two onions boiled till tender and mild, and a few truffles thinly sliced.
- ✓ Pour over a fine salad mixture, and arrange it into a shape, high in center, and garnish with hard eggs cut in slices. A little cucumber mixed with salad is a choice.
- ✓ The mixture may either be a common salad mixture or made as follows: take yolks of three hard boiled eggs, with a spoonful of mustard, and a little salt, mix these with a cup of cream, 4 tablespoonsful of vinegar, different ingredients should be added carefully and worked together smoothly, the whites of the eggs may be trimmed and placed in small heaps round the dish as a garnish.

Tuna Fish Salad

A salad that is both attractive and appetizing can be made by using tuna fish as foundation. This fish, which is grayish white in color, can be obtained in cans like salmon. As it is not high in price, it gives housewife another opportunity to provide her family with an inexpensive protein dish.

Ingredients:

- ✓ 1 can tuna fish
- ✓ 1/2 can diced celery
- ✓ 1 can diced cucumber
- ✓ Salt and pepper
- ✓ Vinegar
- ✓ Lettuce
- ✓ Mayonnaise

Preparation:

- ✓ Open a can of tuna fish, measure 1 cupful, and place in a bowl.
- ✓ Dice the celery and cucumber, mix with the fish, and sprinkle with salt and pepper.

- ✓ Dilute some vinegar with water, using half as much water as vinegar, and sprinkle enough of this over the mixture to flavor it slightly.
- ✓ Allow the mixture to stand for about 1/2 hour in a refrigerator or some other cold place and just before serving pour off this liquid.
- ✓ Heap the salad on lettuce leaves, pour a spoonful of mayonnaise over each portion, and serve.

Salmon Salad

Persons who are fond of salmon will find a salmon salad a very agreeable dish. In addition to affording the means of varying diet, this salad makes a comparatively cheap high-protein dish that is suitable for either supper or luncheon.

Ingredients:

- ✓ 2 c. salmon
- ✓ 1 c. diced celery
- ✓ 1/4 c. diced Spanish onion
- ✓ 3 or 4 sweet pickles, chopped fine
- ✓ French dressing, salad dressing, lettuce

Preparation:

- ✓ Look salmon over carefully, removing any skin and bones. Break into medium-sized pieces and mix carefully with the celery, onion, chopped pickles.
- ✓ Marinate this with the French dressing, taking care not to break up the salmon.
- ✓ Drain and serve with any desired salad dressing on salad plates garnished with lettuce.

Mackerel Salad

Preparation:

- ✓ Pour boiling water over a large mackerel and let stand for ten minutes; take out and dry thoroughly by draining on a sieve or clean towel.
- ✓ Remove the head, tail and fins, and skin and bones.
- ✓ Shred the fish finely and mix with 1 onion chopped.
- ✓ Add mustard, vinegar, and pepper to taste.
- ✓ Serve as salad, with young lettuce leaves, and garnish with hard-boiled eggs, sliced.
- ✓ This is a delightful relish with sliced bread, butter.

Sardine Salad

Ingredients:

- ✓ ½ tin Sardines
- ✓ 2 Eggs
- ✓ 1 Lettuce
- ✓ Salad Dressings

Preparation:

- ✓ Split the sardines open and remove the bone.
- ✓ Break some of the lettuce into a bowl, lay on this the sardines.
- ✓ Chop up one of eggs and sprinkle over them, pour on the dressing.
- ✓ Cover with rest of lettuce, and garnish with the other egg cut in slices, and a little watercress or beetroot.

Crab Salad #1

Preparation:

- ✓ Boil 3 dozen hard-shell crabs twenty-five minutes.
- ✓ Drain and let them cool gradually.
- ✓ Remove upper shell and tail, break remainder apart and pick out the meat carefully.
- ✓ The large claws should not be forgotten, for they contain a dainty morsel, and the creamy fat attached to upper shell should not be overlooked.
- ✓ Line a salad bowl with the small white leaves of two heads of lettuce, add the crab meat, pour over it a "Mayonnaise" garnish with crab claws, hard-boiled eggs, and little mounds of cress leaves, which may be mixed with the salad when served.

Crab Salad #2

Crab meat may be either fresh or canned, but, fresh crab meat is more desirable if it can be obtained.

- ✓ 2 c. crab meat
- ✓ 1 c. diced celery
- ✓ French dressing
- ✓ Lettuce
- ✓ Mayonnaise
- ✓ 1 hard-cooked egg

Preparation:

- ✓ Chill crab meat and add the diced celery.
- ✓ Marinate with French dressing, allow this mixture to stand for ½ hour or so before serving. Keep as cold as possible.
- ✓ Drain off the French dressing and heap the salad mixture on garnished salad plates or in a salad bowl garnished with lettuce.
- ✓ Pour mayonnaise dressing over the top, garnish with slices of hard-cooked egg, and serve.

Shrimp Salad

Shrimps may be used in an attractive salad in the manner. Persons who care for sea food find this an appetizing dish.

Preparation:

- ✓ First marinate shrimps with French dressing and heap them on a plate garnished with lettuce leaves.
- ✓ Add thin slices of hard-cooked egg whites and place a tender heart of celery in the center of the plate.
- ✓ If desired, some slices of celery may be marinated with the shrimp. Serve with mayonnaise dressing.

Prawn Salad

Ingredients:

- ✓ 1-pint Prawns
- ✓ 6 Tomatoes
- ✓ Mayonnaise or Salad Dressing

Preparation:

- ✓ Pick the prawns, leaving the skin on a few fine ones for a garnish.
- ✓ Peel and slice up tomatoes and arrange them on a dish.
- ✓ Put over them the prawns and pour over all some mayonnaise or salad dressing.
- ✓ Place the other prawns round as a garnish with a few lettuce leaves broken up.

MEAT SALADS

Chicken salad #1

The favored means of using left-over chicken is to make a salad of it. It is well, however, if chicken can be prepared especially for the salad and the nicer pieces of meat used. This is usually done when chicken salad is to be served at a party or special dinner.

Ingredients:

- ✓ 2 c. chicken
- ✓ 1 c. diced celery
- ✓ 1 green pepper
- ✓ French dressing
- ✓ Lettuce
- ✓ Mayonnaise
- ✓ 1 pimiento

Preparation:
- ✓ Cut the meat from the bones of a chicken and dice it.
- ✓ Dice celery, clean green pepper, and cut it into small pieces. Mix pepper and celery with the chicken.
- ✓ Marinate with French dressing, chill, allow to stand for about 1/2 hour.

- ✓ Drain the dressing from the salad mixture, serve in a garnished salad bowl or on garnished salad plates, pour mayonnaise over the top.
- ✓ Garnish with strips of pimiento.

Chicken Salad #2

Ingredients:

- ✓ 1 fowl (boiled)
- ✓ 1 cucumber
- ✓ 2 heads lettuce
- ✓ 2 beets (boiled)

Preparation:

- ✓ Dressing made according to the following recipe: 1 teaspoonful mixed mustard + 1 and ½ teaspoonful sugar + 4 tablespoonfuls salad oil + 4 tablespoonfuls milk + 2 tablespoonfuls vinegar; cayenne and salt to taste. Add the oil, drop by drop, to the mustard and sugar, mixing carefully. Then add milk and vinegar gradually, lest the sauce curdle, and the seasoning.
- ✓ Place shredded chicken on a bed of lettuce and pour dressing over it.
- ✓ Around the edge arrange rings of hard-boiled eggs, sliced cucumber and beet root.

Chicken Salad #3

Ingredients:

- ✓ The remains of cold roast or boiled chicken
- ✓ 2 lettuces
- ✓ a little endive
- ✓ 1 cucumber
- ✓ a few slices of boiled beetroot
- ✓ salad-dressing

Preparation:

- ✓ Trim neatly remains of the chicken; wash, dry, and slice lettuces, and place in the middle of a dish.
- ✓ Put the pieces of fowl on the top and pour the salad-dressing over them.
- ✓ Garnish the edge of salad with hard-boiled eggs cut in rings, sliced cucumber, boiled beetroot in slices.
- ✓ Instead of cutting the eggs in rings, the yolks may be rubbed through a hair sieve, and the whites chopped very finely, and arranged on salad in small bunches, yellow and white alternately.

Chicken Salad #4

As an Irishman would say, turkey makes the best chicken salad.

Preparation:

- ✓ Boil till well done. Use only white meat, which cut with sharp scissors into pieces about one-half inch square; add an equal quantity of celery cut in same manner, sprinkling over it salt and pepper.
- ✓ Put in a cold place till two hours before serving, add the following dressing: for 1 chicken take 3 eggs, one cup of vinegar, one cup of sweet milk, ½ cup butter, 1 tablespoon made mustard, salt, black pepper, beat eggs, melt butter; stir all together over a slow fire till it thickens; when cool beat into it one cup of cream.
- ✓ Serve salad on crisp, well-bleached lettuce leaves, on top of each putting a small quantity of mayonnaise dressing.

Southern Chicken Salad

Preparation:

- ✓ Cut one chicken into small pieces (not too small).
- ✓ Boil 1 egg hard and pulverize the yolk (cut white into the chicken).
- ✓ Add beaten yolks of 3 raw eggs; ½ teaspoonful each of ground mustard, white pepper, salt, sugar, celery salt or seed, juice of 1 lemon, 1 tablespoonful melted butter and 1 tablespoonful salad oil. Beat all together until light and pour into one gill of boiling vinegar and let all cook until thick as cream, stirring to avoid curdling.
- ✓ When cold, pour over chicken, to which has been added as much chopped celery, salt and pepper.

Chicken Salad (Hawaiian)

This recipe is good for a summer lunch. You should keep it cold until serving, but mayonnaise is not dangerous, from a food safety point of view. The mayonnaise is acid enough to be protective against bad microorganisms. But it is not protective enough, so do not take chances; do keep this refrigerated until you need it.

Ingredients:

- ✓ 6 cups cooked chicken, cut in chunks
- ✓ 1 ½ cups mayonnaise or salad dressing
- ✓ 2 cups chopped celery
- ✓ 2 tablespoons soy sauce
- ✓ 1 can pineapple tidbits, drained
- ✓ ½ cup slivered almonds, lightly toasted, divided

Preparation:

- ✓ In a large mixing bowl combine the mayonnaise, chicken, celery, soy sauce.
- ✓ Gently fold in pineapple and ½ of almond slivers.
- ✓ Serve it on a platter lined with lettuce. Garnish with almonds.

Chicken Spring Salad

Spinach is an excellent source of Vitamins A and C, as well as potassium and magnesium. When you eat it uncooked, as in this recipe, dentists say spinach is a detergent food, helpful to dental health.

Ingredients:

- ✓ 3 cups cooked chicken, cut in chunks
- ✓ 1 package (10-ounces) raw spinach, washed and drained with stems removed and torn into small pieces
- ✓ 1 small clove garlic, minced
- ✓ 1 tablespoon chives, snipped, fresh or frozen
- ✓ 1 teaspoon salt, 1/8 teaspoon ground pepper
- ✓ 1 teaspoon sugar
- ✓ 3/4 cup chopped pecans
- ✓ 2 apples, chopped
- ✓ ½ cup oil, ¼ cup red wine vinegar

Preparation:
- ✓ In a salad bowl combine all ingredients, toss lightly.
- ✓ Serves 6 to 8.

French Dressing Chicken Salad

This is a real fast food, perfect for when you have got a lot of other things to do besides fuss in the kitchen.

It is quick and easy, but the Cayenne pepper gives it a little perk that lifts it out of the ordinary.

Ingredients:

- ✓ 2 cups cooked, diced chicken
- ✓ 1/2 cup finely chopped celery
- ✓ 1/4 cup French dressing
- ✓ 1/4 cup mayonnaise or salad dressing
- ✓ 1/8 teaspoon Cayenne pepper

Preparation:

- ✓ In a salad bowl toss together all ingredients.
- ✓ Serve on lettuce.
- ✓ Serves 3-4.

Olivey Chicken Salad

Ingredients:

- ✓ 2 cups cooked, diced chicken
- ✓ 1 cup cooked rice (1/4 cup uncooked yields 1 cup cooked)
- ✓ 3/4 cup chopped celery
- ✓ 1/2 cup sliced pimento-stuffed green olives
- ✓ 1/4 cup toasted slivered almonds
- ✓ 1/4 cup thinly sliced scallions
- ✓ 1 teaspoon salt or to taste
- ✓ 1/4 teaspoon ground pepper
- ✓ 1/2 cup mayonnaise or salad dressing
- ✓ 2 tablespoons fresh lemon juice

Preparation:

- ✓ In a mixing bowl combine all ingredients and serve salad on a bed of lettuce leaves.
- ✓ Serves 4 to 6.

Sunshine Chicken Salad

The avocado you use in this recipe should be fully ripe, and that means it will have a slight give to it when you press it between your palms. If it has about as much "give" to it as a baseball, let it ripen for two days at room temperature. Do not refrigerate it: refrigeration puts permanent stop to all ripening.

Ingredients:

- ✓ 3 cups cooked, diced chicken
- ✓ 1 can (6-ounces) orange juice concentrate
- ✓ 3 tablespoons oil
- ✓ 1 tablespoon vinegar
- ✓ 1 tablespoon sugar
- ✓ 1/4 teaspoon dry mustard
- ✓ 1/4 teaspoon salt or to taste
- ✓ 1/8 teaspoon Tabasco
- ✓ 1 cup chopped celery
- ✓ 1/2 cup diced ripe olives
- ✓ 1 medium avocado, cut in small chunks
- ✓ 1/4 cup toasted, slivered almonds

Preparation:

- ✓ In a blender make dressing by blending orange juice, oil, vinegar, sugar, dry mustard, salt and Tabasco at high speed 5 seconds or until smooth.
- ✓ In a salad bowl combine chicken, celery, olives, avocado and almonds. Pour dressing over.
- ✓ Toss and chill at least 30 minutes before serving.
- ✓ Serves 4 to 5.

Corned Beef Salad

Ingredients:

- ✓ Slices of Corned Beef
- ✓ 1 Lettuce
- ✓ 2 Eggs
- ✓ Mayonnaise or Salad Dressing

Preparation:

- ✓ Take some slices of cold corned beef, dip them in a salad dressing, and lay them in a dish with alternate layers of lettuce leaves.
- ✓ Garnish with hard boiled eggs cut in slices.

Mutton Carrot Salad

Ingredients:

- ✓ 2 or 3 Cold Boiled Carrots
- ✓ 1/2 lb. Cold Boiled Mutton
- ✓ 1 stalk Celery
- ✓ 6 Capers
- ✓ ½ teaspoonful Parsley
- ✓ Salad Dressing

Preparation:

- ✓ Cut up some cold boiled mutton into small pieces and lay them in a salad bowl.
- ✓ Mince up celery and capers and strew over it, then pour over the dressing.
- ✓ Slice up the cold carrots and lay them on top.
- ✓ Garnish with the chopped parsley and serve.

Soup Meat Salad

Do you know that boiled meat for soup makes nice salad?

Preparation:
- ✓ When the stock has been poured off, press the meat into a basin with about a gill of jelly stock, and some salt and pepper. When cold and firm, cut it into neat pieces and lay in a salad bowl.
- ✓ Pour over it some remoulade sauce and shred on top some nice white lettuce leaves.
- ✓ It may be garnished with beetroot, hard-boiled eggs.

Lamb Salad

Ingredients:

- ✓ Cold Roast Lamb
- ✓ 2 Lettuces
- ✓ 1 Tomato
- ✓ 12 Capers
- ✓ 2 Eggs
- ✓ Remoulade Dressing

Preparation:

- ✓ Cut the lamb into small pieces and lay it in a bowl.
- ✓ Cut the tomato into thin slices and lay it over, then the capers chopped small.
- ✓ Pour over the dressing, break up the lettuces and put over, and garnish with the hard-boiled eggs cut in slices.

Italian Meat Salad #1

Ingredients:

- ✓ 1 Salt Herring
- ✓ Cold slices of Meat
- ✓ 1 teaspoonful Mustard
- ✓ 1 Beetroot
- ✓ 4 tablespoonsful Oil
- ✓ 3 tablespoonsful Tarragon Vinegar
- ✓ 1/2 oz. Capers
- ✓ 3 Boiled Potatoes

Preparation:

- ✓ Wash herring in cold water and soak it in milk for an hour; cut it open and take-out bone and slice up both the fish and the meat.
- ✓ Arrange in a bowl, chop the capers, and put over.
- ✓ Put mustard into a basin, add gradually oil, vinegar.
- ✓ Pour this, when well mixed, over fish and meat, and cover with slices of cold potatoes.
- ✓ Garnish with any cold vegetables in larder.

Italian Meat Salad #2

Preparation:

- ✓ Cut up the white parts of a cold fowl, and mix it with mustard and cress, and a lettuce chopped finely, and mix with a fine salad mixture, composed of the same quantities of vinegar, salad, oil, salt, mustard, yolks of hard-boiled eggs, and yolk of one raw egg.
- ✓ A little tarragon vinegar is then added, and mixture is poured over the salad.
- ✓ The whites of eggs are mixed, and serve to garnish the dish, arranged in small heaps alternately with heaps of grated smoked beef.
- ✓ 2 or 3 hard boiled eggs are cut up with the chicken in small pieces and mixed with salad.
- ✓ The appearance of this salad may be varied by piling the fowl in the center of the dish, then pour over the salad mixture, and make a wall of any dressed salad, laying the whites of eggs (after the yolks have been removed for the mixture), cut in rings on the top like a chain.

Grouse Salad

Ingredients:

- ✓ 8 eggs
- ✓ Butter
- ✓ Fresh salad
- ✓ 1 or 2 grouse

Preparation:

- ✓ Boil eggs hard, shell them, throw them into cold water, cut a thin slice off the bottom to facilitate the proper placing of them in dish, cut each one into four lengthwise and make a very thin flat border of butter, about 1 inch from the edge of the dish the salad is to be served on.
- ✓ Fix the pieces of egg upright close to each other, the yolk outside, or the yolk and white alternately.
- ✓ Lay in center a fresh salad and, having previously roasted grouse rather underdone, cut it into eight or ten pieces, and prepare the sauce as follows:

- ✓ <u>For sauce:</u> 1 teaspoonful of minced shalot, 1 teaspoonful of pounded sugar, yolk of 1 egg, 1 teaspoonful of minced parsley, 1/4 oz. of salt, 4 tablespoonfuls of oil, 2 tablespoonfuls of Chili vinegar, 1 gill of cream.

- ✓ Put the shalots into a basin, with the sugar, the yolk of an egg, the parsley, and salt, and mix in by degrees the oil and vinegar.
- ✓ When these ingredients are well mixed, put sauce on ice or in a cool place. When ready to serve, whip the cream rather thick, which lightly mix with it; then lay the inferior parts of grouse on salad, sauce over to cover each piece, lay over salad and remainder of grouse, pour the sauce and serve.
- ✓ Eggs may be ornamented with a little dot of radishes or beetroot on the point. Anchovy and gherkin, cut into small diamonds, may be placed between, or cut gherkins in slices, and a border of them laid round.

OTHER SALADS

Bread salad

Ingredients:

- ✓ 5 slices Stale Bread
- ✓ 1/2 gill Oil
- ✓ 3 Pickled Onions
- ✓ 1 piece Pickled Cauliflower
- ✓ 2 Eggs
- ✓ 1 Beetroot
- ✓ 2 slices Cold Mutton
- ✓ 1 tablespoonful Vinegar
- ✓ Mustard and Cress

Preparation:

- ✓ Trim off crust and cut the bread into dice, put into a bowl and pour over the oil. Let it stand till all the oil is absorbed.
- ✓ Mince up onion, cauliflower, eggs, meat, and strew them over. Season with pepper, salt. Wash mustard and cress and arrange on top. Cut beetroot into neat shapes and arrange as a garnish.

Chestnut Salad

Ingredients:

- ✓ Bananas, apples, celery and chestnuts.

Preparation:

- ✓ Equal parts of boiled chestnuts and shredded celery are combined.
- ✓ Dress with mayonnaise and serve on lettuce leaves.

Sweetbread Salad

Preparation:

- ✓ Take cucumbers, cut lengthwise to serve salad in.
- ✓ Scrape out the inside and salt well, then squeeze and use this to mix with the filling.
- ✓ Take a pair of sweetbreads, or calf's brains, wash and boil. When done, throw in cold water, skim them.
- ✓ Chop fine, add bunch of celery, one can of French peas, scraped part of cucumber; mix all together and season. Make a mayonnaise, mix with it, fill cucumber shells.
- ✓ Keep all cold and serve on lettuce leaf.

Neapolitan Salad

Ingredients:

- ✓ Some white meat of a turkey (cut up fine, cut up a few pickles the same way)
- ✓ A few beets
- ✓ 1 or 2 carrots (parboiled)
- ✓ A few potatoes (parboiled)
- ✓ A few stalks of asparagus
- ✓ Chop up a bunch of crisp
- ✓ White celery
- ✓ A whole celery root (parboiled)

Preparation:

- ✓ Sprinkle all with fine salt and pour a mayonnaise dressing over it.
- ✓ Line salad bowl with lettuce leaves or white cabbage leaves.
- ✓ Add a few hard-boiled eggs and capers.
- ✓ Garnish with sprigs of fresh parsley.

Spanish Salad

Preparation:

- ✓ Put into the center of a bowl, cold dressed French beans, or scarlet runners, and before serving pour over some good mayonnaise.
- ✓ Garnish the beans with three tomatoes cut in slices and arranged in a circle one overlapping the other.

VARIOUS SALAD DRESSINGS

Various salad dressings may be made to serve with salads. The kind of dressing to select depends both on the variety of salad served and on the personal preference of those to whom it is served. Some of these contain a few ingredients and are comparatively simple to make; others are complex and involve considerable work in their making.

Whether simple or elaborate, however, the salad dressing should be carefully chosen, so that it will blend well with the ingredients of the salad with which it is used.

Several recipes for salad dressings are here given. They are taken up before the recipes for salads so that the beginner will be familiar with the different varieties when they are mentioned in connection with salads.

As many of the recipes as possible should be tried, not only for knowledge that will be gained, but also for the practical experience.

French Dressing #1

A dressing that is very simply made and that can probably be used with a greater variety of salads is French dressing.

Preparation:

- ✓ Mix 1 tablespoon of lemon juice or vinegar, 1/2 teaspoon salt, 1/8 teaspoon pepper or few grains cayenne pepper in bowl.
- ✓ Add 3 to 4 tablespoons olive oil, beating constantly.
- ✓ Place on ice until ready to serve.

French Dressing #2

It may be used with any vegetable salad, with salads mixed with fruit, and with meat, fish, and egg salads.

Ingredients:

- ✓ 3/4 tsp. salt
- ✓ 1/4 tsp. mustard
- ✓ 1/4 tsp. pepper
- ✓ 3 Tb. vinegar
- ✓ 1/4 tsp. paprika
- ✓ 1/2 c. oil

Preparation:

- ✓ Measure dry ingredients and place them in a bowl.
- ✓ Measure vinegar, oil, add them to dry ingredients.
- ✓ Beat with a fork until the ingredients are thoroughly mixed and the oil and vinegar form an emulsion that will remain for a short time.
- ✓ Keep cold the ingredients as cold as possible before mixing them.

Cream Salad Dressing #1

A simple dressing that requires very little time or skill in preparation and that affords a means of using up cream that has soured is the one given in the accompanying recipe. Sweet cream may also be used in the same way if desired, and this makes an excellent dressing for cabbage salad, plain cucumber salad with lettuce, or fruit salad. If the dressing is to be used for fruit salad, lemon juice may be used in the place of vinegar.

Ingredients:

- ✓ 1 c. sour cream
- ✓ 1/2 tsp. salt
- ✓ 2 Tb. sugar
- ✓ 1/4 c. vinegar

Preparation:
- ✓ Whip the cream with a rotary beater until it is stiff.
- ✓ Then add the sugar, salt, vinegar; continue beating until the mixture is well blended.
- ✓ Cool and serve.

Cream Salad Dressing #2

Ingredients:

- ✓ Two eggs
- ✓ Three table-spoonfuls of vinegar
- ✓ One of cream
- ✓ One teaspoonful of sugar
- ✓ One-fourth of a teaspoonful of salt
- ✓ One-fourth of a teaspoonful of mustard.

Preparation:

- ✓ Beat two eggs well. Add the sugar, salt and mustard, then the vinegar, and the cream.
- ✓ Place the bowl in a basin of boiling water, stir until about the thickness of rich cream.
- ✓ If the bowl is thick and water boils all the time, it will take about 5 minutes.
- ✓ Cool, and use as needed.

Sour Cream Dressing #1

Sour-cream dressing is not very cheap to make. It is, however, a very good dressing for both fruit and vegetable salad.

Ingredients:
- ✓ 2 Tb. butter
- ✓ 1/3 c. vinegar
- ✓ 3 Tb. flour
- ✓ 1 c. sour cream
- ✓ 2 Tb. Sugar, 1 tsp. salt
- ✓ 2 eggs
- ✓ 1 c. whipped cream

Preparation:
- ✓ Melt butter in the upper part of a double boiler, add flour, sugar, salt, vinegar, and sour cream.
- ✓ Cook together over flame until the mixture thickens.
- ✓ Beat egg yolks, add them to this. Place in the lower part of the double boiler and cook until the egg yolks thicken. Beat the egg whites and fold them with the whipped cream into salad dressing. Cool and serve.

Sour Cream Dressing #2

Preparation:

- ✓ Mix one cup of sour cream and 3 eggs, well beaten.
- ✓ Dissolve 2 tablespoons of sugar and 1 tablespoon of mustard in one-half cup of vinegar.
- ✓ Salt, pepper and paprika to taste, then stir slowly into the cream and eggs.
- ✓ Put in double boiler, cook until thick, add butter the size of an egg and cook about five minutes longer.
- ✓ Take from fire and bottle.
- ✓ This dressing will keep for months.

Mayonnaise Dressing #1

Although mayonnaise dressing is prepared without heat, it is not one of the simplest dressings to prepare.

It meets with much favor, being used almost as extensively as French dressing, but it is less desirable with fruit salads than with others. It is much used as a basis for many other dressings.

Before serving, it may be thinned by beating either sweet or sour cream into it. It may be made fluffy and light and its quantity may be increased by beating whipped cream into it.

Ingredients:

- 1/2 tsp. salt
- 2 egg yolks
- 1/4 tsp. pepper
- 1-1/2 c. oil
- 1/4 tsp. mustard
- 4 Tb. vinegar or lemon juice

Preparation:

- ✓ Mix the dry ingredients in a bowl. Separate the eggs and add the yolks to the dry ingredients.
- ✓ Beat these with a rotary eggbeater until they are well mixed. To the mixture, add drops of oil continue to beat. Add a drop of the vinegar or lemon juice, a few more drops of oil, and beat constantly.
- ✓ Gradually increase quantity of oil added each time, but do not do this rapidly. As the oil is added and beating is continued, it will be noted that mixture grows thicker, but when vinegar is added mixture is thinned.
- ✓ Quantity of vinegar is so much less than that of oil that the oil may be added in small amounts two or three times in succession before vinegar is added.
- ✓ This process is rather long and slow, but if the mixing is done correctly, the result will be a smooth mixture that will not separate for possibly 6 days.
- ✓ Mayonnaise may be made with a bowl and a rotary beater, if it will just be remembered that liquid ingredients must be added slowly and that they must be as cold as possible.

Mayonnaise Dressing #2

Ingredients:

- ✓ 1 egg yolk
- ✓ 1/2 teaspoon dry mustard
- ✓ 1/2 teaspoon salt
- ✓ 1/16 teaspoon cayenne pepper
- ✓ 1 cup salad oil
- ✓ 2 tablespoons vinegar or lemon juice

Preparation:

- ✓ Utensils and ingredients should be very cold.
- ✓ Put egg yolk into shallow bowl.
- ✓ Add, seasoning and mix well; add oil slowly, almost drop by drop, beating continually until very thick.
- ✓ Thin with vinegar.
- ✓ Continue adding oil and vinegar until all is used.

Mayonnaise Dressing #3

Ingredients:

- ✓ 1 egg
- ✓ juice of 1 lemon or 4 tablespoons vinegar
- ✓ 1 teaspoon salt
- ✓ 1/4 teaspoon paprika
- ✓ few grains cayenne
- ✓ 2 cups salad oil

Preparation:

- ✓ Put egg with vinegar or lemon juice, seasoning into bowl and beat with rotary eggbeater.
- ✓ Add oil a tablespoonful or more at a time, beating constantly.
- ✓ This mayonnaise will keep for three or four weeks.

Cooked Mayonnaise

A dressing that is very similar both in texture and taste to the mayonnaise just explained and perhaps a little easier to make is known as cooked mayonnaise. This dressing, as will be noted from the accompanying recipe, may be made in larger quantities than the Uncooked mayonnaise.

Ingredients:
- ✓ 2 Tb. oil
- ✓ 1/4 tsp. mustard
- ✓ 4 Tb. flour
- ✓ 1/4 tsp. paprika
- ✓ 1/2 c. vinegar
- ✓ 2 eggs
- ✓ 1 c. boiling water
- ✓ 2 c. oil
- ✓ 1 Tb. salt

Preparation:
- ✓ Mix 2 tablespoonfuls of oil and the flour and pour in the vinegar. Add boiling water and stir mixture until it is perfectly smooth and well mixed.
- ✓ Place over the fire and cook for about 5 minutes.

- ✓ Remove from fire and cool.
- ✓ When completely cooled, add the salt, mustard, and paprika.
- ✓ Separate eggs and beat yolks and whites separately.
- ✓ Add the egg yolks to the mixture.
- ✓ Add 2 cupsful of oil a little at a time, beating thoroughly with a rotary beater each time oil is added. When all of this is completely mixed and thoroughly beaten, fold in the stiffly beaten egg whites.